NAPOLEON BONAPARTE
and Imperial France

by Miriam Greenblatt

 Marshall Cavendish
Benchmark
New York

ACKNOWLEDGMENT

The author and publisher wish to especially thank Katherine Pence, Assistant Professor of European History at Baruch College in New York City, for her thoughtful comments on the manuscript.

Marshall Cavendish Benchmark
99 White Plains Road
Tarrytown, New York 10591-9001
www.marshallcavendish.us

Text copyright © 2006 by Miriam Greenblatt
Map copyright © 2006 by Marshall Cavendish Corporation
Map by Rodica Prato

All Internet sites were available and accurate when this book was sent to press.

Library of Congress Cataloging-in-Publication Data
Greenblatt, Miriam.
Napoleon Bonaparte and Imperial France / by Miriam Greenblatt.
p. cm. — (Rulers and their times)
Includes bibliographical references and index.
ISBN 0-7614-1837-7
1. Napoleon I, Emperor of the French, 1769–1821—Juvenile literature. 2. Emperors—France—Biography—Juvenile literature. 3. France—History—Consulate and First Empire, 1799–1815—Juvenile literature.
I. Title. II. Series.
DC203.G82   2005   944.05′092—dc22   2004022239

Art Research: Rose Corbett Gordon, Mystic CT
Cover: The Art Archive/Fondation Thiers, Paris/Dagli Orti
Photo Credits: Pages 1, 71: Chateau de Versailles, France/Lauros/Giraudon/Bridgeman Art Library; pages 4, 19, 83, 84, 87, 89: The Art Archive/Malmaison Musée du Chateau/Dagli Orti; pages 6–7: Tate Gallery, London/Art Resource, NY; page 9: Alinari/Art Resource, NY; page 10, 11: Musée Antoine Lecuyer, Saint-Quentin, France/Bridgeman Art Library; page 13: Giraudon/Art Resource, NY; page 15: Private Collection/Bridgeman Art Library; pages 17, 23, 54–55, 57, 69, 73: Erich Lessing/Art Resource, NY; page 26: Christie's Images/Corbis; page 28: Bibliothèque des Arts Decoratifs, Paris, France/Archives Charmet/Bridgeman Art Library; pages 30, 33: The Art Archive/Musée du Château de Versailles/Dagli Orti; page 36: The Art Archive/Musée du Louvre/Dagli Orti; page 40: Archivo Iconografico, S.A./Corbis; page 42: Wallace Collection, London/Bridgeman Art Library; page 45: FORBES Magazine Collection, New York/Bridgeman Art Library; page 51: Army and Navy Club, London/Bridgeman Art Library; pages 60, 86: Réunion des Musées Nationaux/Art Resource, NY; page 62: Musée d'Art et d'Industrie, Roubaix, France/Giraudon/Bridgeman Art Library; page 65: Archivo Iconografico, S.A./Corbis; page 77: The Art Archive/Bibliothèque des Arts Décoratifs, Paris/Dagli Orti; pages 78–79: The Art Archive/Musée du Château de Versailles/Dagli Orti

Printed in China
135642

Permission has been granted to use extended quotations from the following copyrighted works:
Daily Life in France under Napoleon, translated by Violet M. MacDonald, 1963, p. 150.
The Horizon Book of the Age of Napoleon, edited by Marshall B. Davidson and J. Christopher Herold, 1963. Reprinted by permission of American Heritage, Inc.
Napoleon and the Napoleonic Wars by Albert Marrin. Copyright © Albert Marrin, 1991. Used by permission of Wendy Schmalz Agency.
The Story of Civilization: Part XI, The Age of Napoleon: A History of European Civilization from 1789 to 1815 by Will and Ariel Durant by permission of Simon and Schuster Adult Publishing Group. Copyright © 1975 by Will and Ariel Durant.

5-1-06

Contents

Gone but Not Forgotten   4

PART ONE: An Ambitious Man   6
    Early Years   8
    The French Revolution   10
    Enter Napoleon   17
    The Italian Campaign   21
    The Egyptian Campaign   25
    Seizing Power   29
    The First Consul   32
    The Empire Expands   35
    The Empire Comes Apart   39
    The "Hundred Days"   49
    Napoleon's Legacy   53

PART TWO: Everyday Life in Napoleonic France   54
    The Military   56
    Education   60
    Earning a Living   62
    Food   64
    Houses and Furniture   67
    Clothes and Makeup   70
    Literature and the Arts   73
    Having Fun   75

PART THREE: The French in Their Own Words   78

Map   46

Glossary   90

For Further Reading   91

Bibliography   92

Notes   93

Index   94

Gone but Not Forgotten

Few individuals in history have captured people's imaginations the way Napoleon has. He has been the subject of tens of thousands of books, more than any other historical personage except Jesus Christ. Little boys everywhere play with toy soldiers dressed in the uniforms of Napoleon's armies. War-games enthusiasts refight his battles on their computers. His life has been commemorated in hundreds of paintings, plays, and motion pictures.

Napoleon at age thirty-five, just before he became emperor of France

In this book, you will read how an outsider born on the island of Corsica rose to be not only emperor of France but also conqueror of most of Europe. You will learn about his marriages, his relationship with his soldiers, and the techniques he used to keep his power. You will learn, too, about the way the French people lived: the foods they ate, the clothes they wore, and what they did for entertainment. Finally, you will read some letters, diary entries, newspaper headlines, and personal advertisements that provide a closer glimpse into the thoughts and concerns of Napoleon and his subjects.

PART ONE

Napoleon dreamed of conquering
Europe and leading his nation to
great heights. Events, as history
would show, did not turn out
quite the way he hoped.

An Ambitious Man

Early Years

Napoleon Bonaparte was born on the island of Corsica on August 15, 1769. The island, which lies in the Mediterranean Sea between France and Italy, had been controlled by the Italian city of Genoa since the 1300s. In 1768, Genoa sold the island to France. That made Napoleon a French citizen when he was born. His first language, however, was Italian, and he always spoke French with a strong Corsican accent.

When Napoleon was ten, his father—a moderately well-to-do lawyer and a member of the Corsican nobility—obtained a scholarship for him at the royal military academy at Brienne-le-Château in France. Napoleon studied at Brienne for five years, from 1779 to 1784. It was an unhappy time. He was shy and unsociable, and his fellow students made fun of his short stature and sallow complexion.

Life improved somewhat as Napoleon became older. When he was fifteen, he was chosen to attend the École Militaire in Paris. An avid student who loved to read, he completed the course in one year instead of the usual two. He shone at math, geography, and history, but did poorly in German, dancing, music, and social skills. One of his teachers described him as being "quiet and solitary, capricious [changeable], haughty, and frightfully egotistical. He replies energetically to questions in class and is swift and sharp in his repartee at other times. He is most proud, ambitious, aspiring to everything."

Napoleon was born in this house in Ajaccio, Corsica. He was the fourth child and second son of his parents. In all, the elder Bonapartes had thirteen children, eight of whom lived to adulthood.

In 1785, at the age of sixteen, Napoleon was commissioned a second lieutenant in an artillery regiment of the French army. Since France was then at peace, life in the army was relaxed and easy. The young lieutenant had plenty of time in which to read books, see plays, discover women, and visit Corsica on leave. He also assumed the responsibility of supporting his mother and seven brothers and sisters after his father died.

Then, in 1789, the French Revolution broke out, and Napoleon's life changed completely.

The French Revolution

To understand how Napoleon was able to accomplish what he did, it helps to know something about French history.

For hundreds of years, France had been a monarchy whose king ruled by divine right. That is, he ruled because God had supposedly given him the right to do so. Below the king were three estates, or classes: the clergy, the nobles, and the common people.

The nobles held almost all the high offices in the government and the army. They also held the higher offices of the Roman Catholic Church, such as archbishops and bishops. (Catholicism was France's official religion.) Some nobles lived on large estates worked by peasants. Other nobles lived at court, where they did little except attend balls and banquets and try to outdo one another in the elegance of their clothes. Nobles who held church

Marie-Antoinette, the Austrian princess who married Louis XVI, had great beauty and style. On the other hand, she was poorly educated, frivolous, and very extravagant. The royal couple wed when she was fourteen and he was fifteen.

offices likewise lived luxurious lives. Usually, only the hardworking parish priests carried out their religious obligations.

The clergy and nobles were exempt from most taxes. As a result, almost the entire tax burden fell on the Third Estate—the peasants, artisans, tradespeople, and professionals. This economic imbalance was reflected in the French parliament, known as the Estates-General, in which each class had one vote. In other words, even though ordinary French people made up more than 95 percent of the population, they could be outvoted by the First and Second Estates, the clergy and nobles.

In 1789, the French king, Louis XVI, convened the Estates-General in order to pass new tax laws. (The French parliament, unlike legislative bodies today, only met at the pleasure of the monarch.) Louis needed more revenue, in large part because of the cost of helping the Americans in their recent war for independence against Great Britain, France's ancient enemy. When the Estates-General met, however, the delegates to the Third Estate—inspired by new political ideas about liberty and human rights that were taking root in western Europe—called for a change in the voting rules. Instead of one class–one vote, they wanted one man–one vote. This would enable the common people to outvote the

Unlike his wife, Louis XVI was well educated. He knew physics and mathematics and spoke several languages. He also enjoyed hunting and working on carpentry.

nobles and clergy. The latter naturally refused to go along with the idea. The delegates of the Third Estate then declared themselves the National Assembly, representing all of France. Shortly thereafter, they were locked out of their meeting room in the parliament. Determined to prevail, the members reassembled in a nearby indoor tennis court, where they were joined by several members of the First and Second Estates. They vowed that they would not disband until they had written a constitution for France. The pledge they made later became known as the Oath of the Tennis Court.

Meanwhile, Louis could not decide what to do. One day he seemed to support the Assembly. The next day he ordered troops to gather outside Paris. Finally, his hand was forced. On July 14, 1789, an armed group of artisans and tradespeople stormed the Bastille, an old fortress that housed political prisoners as well as a large supply of gunpowder. The mob killed many of the defending soldiers, beheaded the Bastille's governor, seized the gunpowder, and freed the seven prisoners inside. Ever since, France has celebrated Bastille Day just as the United States celebrates the Fourth of July.

A Constitutional Monarchy

The fall of the Bastille was followed by several successive changes in government.

The Assembly began by issuing a document similar to the Bill of Rights of the U.S. Constitution. It was called the Declaration of the Rights of Man and of the Citizen. Among other things, it stated that all citizens were equal before the law and that every citizen might "speak, write, and print with freedom."

Many French artists have depicted the storming of the Bastille on July 14, 1789. One reason for the attack's success was the fact that many of the French soldiers defending the prison would not fire on the attackers.

Using the Declaration as a guideline, the Assembly in 1791 established a constitutional monarchy. Under it, the king's powers were limited and the legislature was to meet regularly. (Before 1789, the Estates General had not met for 175 years!)

The issuance of the Declaration and the change in France's government alarmed the rulers of Austria and Prussia. What if *their* subjects decided to change their governments along similar lines? The rulers of Austria and Prussia also saw an opportunity to expand their territories. So the two nations signed a military alliance against France with the aim of restoring its king by force. France responded by declaring war.

The First French Republic

At first the professional armies of Austria and Prussia were victorious. Then the French armies—which consisted mostly of volunteers who felt they were fighting for liberty as well as their country's future—defeated the invaders. In the meantime, the French monarchy was abolished and replaced with a republic headed by an elected National Convention. A few months later, the Convention accused the former king of treason for having encouraged foreign troops to invade France. The Convention put him on trial, found him guilty, and sentenced him to death by the guillotine.

At this point, England and Spain joined the war against France. The Convention then formed a Committee of Public Safety to take charge of affairs at home and abroad. The Committee consisted of the most radical leaders of the Convention. The most famous—or infamous, depending on which historian you read—was Maximilien Robespierre. Determined to remake French society in the interests of the common man, Robespierre ordered three years of free, compulsory education for everyone. He also abolished slavery in France's overseas colonies and did away with imprisonment for debt. On the other hand, he would not tolerate any opposition. He began a campaign to eliminate not only royalists (people who supported a monarchy), but also anyone who criticized the government. Trials were swift, and the accused often could not present any evidence in their defense. Historians estimate that between 25,000 and 50,000 people were beheaded during the bloody period known as the Reign of Terror.

The Directory

By 1794, the moderate members of the National Convention had had their fill of domestic bloodshed. They wanted no more mass executions of French citizens. They guillotined Robespierre and in

The guillotine was named after Dr. Joseph Guillotin, who recommended the device as a quick and merciful means of execution.

1795 wrote a new constitution establishing a different form of republic. It was to be headed by a group of five men called the Directory, assisted by a two-house legislature. Both royalists and radical supporters of the republic, however, were more or less excluded from membership in the legislature. So the two groups decided to stage a coup d'état and overthrow the government.

At midnight on October 3, 1795, thousands of armed royalists, together with members of the working class, began marching through the streets of Paris. Their goal was the Tuileries, the palace where the Convention was housed. They were in position as dawn broke.

Enter Napoleon

During the first four years of the revolution, Napoleon spent much of his time in Corsica. In June 1793, he was forced to flee the island because he opposed a group of Corsicans who were seeking independence. Taking his mother, brothers, and sisters with him, he landed in southern France.

A few months later, he was promoted to major and given command of the republican forces attacking the naval base of Toulon. It was not an enviable assignment. Toulon was held by a combination of royalists and British soldiers, while British and Spanish ships filled the city's harbor. The republican troops trying to capture Toulon were poorly armed and short of supplies.

This is the first portrait ever made of Napoleon. It shows him as the commander in chief of the French army fighting in Italy.

The unfavorable odds did not daunt Napoleon. On the contrary: here was an opportunity for him to show what he could do. First, he rode through the surrounding countryside and seized all the guns, ammunition, food, and horses he could find. Next, he positioned all his cannons so as to direct their fire at the fort overlooking Toulon. After several days' bombardment, the fort fell. Napoleon then turned the fort's guns around and began bombarding the Anglo-Spanish battle fleet in Toulon's harbor. The British and Spanish withdrew—and in December 1793 Napoleon was promoted to brigadier general.

Eight months later, in August 1794, Napoleon found himself in jail, charged with conspiracy and treason because he had been friendly with Robespierre's brother. He was soon released. But instead of receiving another army command, he was put in charge of the government's map-making office.

Despite this setback to his ambition, Napoleon was deliriously happy. After two failed relationships, he had fallen in love. Her name was Marie-Josèphe-Rose de Beauharnais. Napoleon called her Josephine. Six years older than himself, Josephine was a widow whose late husband had been guillotined during the Reign of Terror. She was beautiful, witty, elegant—and a spendthrift. In fact, one of the reasons she flirted with Napoleon at first was that she thought he was rich. Ironically, Napoleon was under the impression that *she* was rich.

At the time the two met, Josephine was the mistress of Paul de Barras, a leading member of the National Convention. Napoleon and Barras had known each other for about two years. Each now saw a way to make use of the other. Napoleon was looking for a powerful person who could help advance his career. Barras, who had been put in charge of defending Paris against both foreign attacks and local mobs, needed a military man on whom to rely since he himself had no battle experience.

On October 3, 1795, as rumors of the royalist-radical uprising swept through Paris, Barras met with Napoleon, who agreed to defend the government against the mob. Following the tactics that had proved successful at Toulon, he sent for all the cannons he

When Josephine and Napoleon wed, they both fibbed on the marriage license. She lowered her age by four years, while he raised his age by one year.

could get and placed them at strategic points in front of a church near the Tuileries.

The rebels launched their first attack on the morning of October 4 but were unable to advance. That afternoon, they launched a second attack. After considerable fighting, the government troops in front of the Tuileries succeeded in pushing the rebels toward the church where Napoleon was waiting. As the mob neared, Napoleon gave the order to fire. The shots from his heavy cannons swept through the rebel ranks, leaving hundreds of corpses lying on the ground. The rebels fled for their lives— and the government was saved.

Both Barras and Napoleon were now heroes. Within a few weeks, Barras became one of the five members of the newly formed Directory. Napoleon was promoted to major general and put in charge of all troops within France. Three months after that, he finally received an active military command. He was to head the French army fighting in Italy.

On March 6, 1796, Napoleon and Josephine were married. Two days later, he left for Italy. His path to glory had begun.

The Italian Campaign

Italy at that time was not a unified nation but rather a collection of separate states. Many of them were ruled, either directly or indirectly, by Austria. The Directory hoped that attacking these states would put pressure on Austria and force it to sign a peace treaty with France.

When Napoleon arrived in Italy, he found a demoralized French army that had not been paid in months and that lacked both food and ammunition. Napoleon promptly scoured the neighborhood and managed to scrounge up enough food and brandy to last his soldiers about one week. Next, he delivered the first of a series of stirring speeches to his troops: "Soldiers! You are ill-fed and almost naked. The government owes you a great deal, but it can do nothing for you. Your patience and courage do you honor but give you neither worldly goods nor glory. I shall lead you into the most fertile plains on earth. There you shall find great cities and rich provinces. There you shall find honor, glory, riches. Soldiers of the Army of Italy! Could courage and constancy possibly fail you?"

Napoleon then adopted a course of action he would follow many times in the future. He marched his troops rapidly and split the enemy forces in two. After defeating one army, he turned and smashed the second army. Napoleon understood that a decisive general with well-motivated soldiers would be able to defeat slower troops even if they were much more numerous.

It was a short time later, during another battle against the Austrians, that Napoleon received his nickname "the Little Corporal." The French army had run into heavy fire while attacking across a wooden bridge. Napoleon rushed forward to lead the French soldiers. Since it was customary for corporals rather than generals to lead troops into battle, Napoleon's soldiers were thrilled by his action, and their devotion to their commander increased tremendously.

As Napoleon moved through Italy, he presented himself as a liberator. "Peoples of Italy! The French army comes to break your chains. The French nation is the friend of all nations; receive us with trust! Your property, your religion, your customs will be respected. We shall wage war like generous enemies, for our only quarrel is with the tyrants who have enslaved you."

Napoleon's words were impressive. The reality, however, was quite different. The French looted the Italian cities they conquered and sent thousands of wagons loaded with gold, silver, and especially paintings and other works of art to Paris. Things became so bad that Italians in various parts of the peninsula actually revolted against the French "liberation." The revolts were suppressed.

In October 1797, Napoleon signed a peace treaty with Austria. He had not been authorized by the Directory to do so, but the French people did not care. They gave him a tumultuous welcome when he returned to Paris in December.

This upset the members of the Directory. The French government was on shaky ground. It had failed to solve the country's food

Napoleon's conquest of Venice ended more than a thousand years of that city's independence. This monumental arch was built to mark the Little Corporal's Venetian triumph.

shortages, control inflation, or provide jobs for the unemployed. Many people had started murmuring that perhaps Louis XVI had not been so bad after all. Suppose the war hero decided to overthrow the Directory and seize power for himself?

The Directory's solution was to give Napoleon the task of invading England. At the very least, it would get him out of Paris. Furthermore, with the defeat of Austria, England was now France's greatest enemy.

Napoleon rejected the Directory's idea. He pointed out that the British navy controlled the English Channel and would easily destroy an invasion fleet. Besides, the French did not have enough ships to move the necessary men and supplies to England. Instead, Napoleon proposed an invasion of Egypt. (Egypt was then part of the Turkish-run Ottoman Empire, which was friendly to Britain.) Conquering Egypt would interfere with British trade in the Middle East. The country was also a potential base for a future French attack on India, the "crown jewel" of the British Empire. The Directory agreed, and in May 1798 Napoleon set sail for Egypt.

The Egyptian Campaign

Unlike Napoleon's Italian campaign, his Egyptian campaign was a military disaster. Napoleon was a superb tactician, but he failed to consider the effects of climate and geography. He also failed to plan the Egyptian campaign properly. He had no idea where the main food storage depots and wells along his proposed invasion route were located. Yet he did not bring along extra supplies of food or water. Nor did he bring the horses, donkeys, and oxen that would be needed to move his cannons and supplies. He thought he would be able to live off the land. He did not take into account the fact that most of Egypt was a barren desert and that he was invading during the hottest month of the year.

Despite these obstacles, Napoleon managed to capture the main Egyptian cities of Alexandria and Cairo. He then suffered a major defeat at sea. A British fleet commanded by Admiral Horatio Nelson attacked the French ships anchored at Abu Qir Bay near Alexandria and captured or destroyed almost every one. The French were now cut off from home and unable to receive reinforcements of food, supplies, or men.

While Napoleon was considering what to do next, some of his soldiers, at work rebuilding a fort, made an extraordinary discovery. They found a black rock on which was carved a single message in

Napoleon appears every inch the hero in this painting of him on the Egyptian campaign. The truth, as it turned out, was another matter.

three different scripts. The rock would come to be called the Rosetta Stone, after the village in which it was found, and it would open the door to our knowledge of ancient Egypt.

The rock was eventually placed in the hands of scholars who puzzled over it for more than two decades. One of the three scripts was in the

Greek language, which scholars understood. The other two scripts represented two different ways to write the ancient Egyptian language, namely, hieroglyphic (picture writing) and demotic (a cursive, or flowing, form of Egyptian hieroglyphs). By comparing the Greek script with the hieroglyphs, one of the scholars, Jean-François Champollion, was able to decipher the hieroglyphs, and the ancient Egyptian world came alive.

But right now the ancient Egyptians were not Napoleon's concern. He and his army had been in Egypt for nine months. Cut off from all assistance thanks to the British navy, the general had to figure a way out. His solution was to move east and launch an invasion of Palestine and Syria. (Like Egypt, they were then part of the Ottoman Empire.) Although he won some victories against the Turks, he failed to capture the city of Acre. This defeat, combined with the blazing heat, forced him to return to Cairo. By this time, he had lost one-third of his army to wounds, syphilis, and bubonic plague. He was short of money with which to pay his troops, and many of his officers had requested permission to return to France. In addition, the British were landing fresh Turkish troops all along the Egyptian coast. It was only a matter of time before the combined British and Turkish forces would launch a decisive attack against the French.

In August 1799, Napoleon deserted his army and sailed for home. A thick fog enabled him to avoid the British blockade, and he landed in France in October. He was received as a conquering hero, for the reports he had been sending back told only about his victories. It took more than two years for news of his defeat to reach France, and by then the truth no longer mattered. The French troops he left behind surrendered to the British in 1801. Most were later exchanged for British prisoners held by the French

Napoleon sails
back to France
from Egypt.

and were returned home. Although they continued to serve in France's army, "the vast majority would never," as one historian wrote, "forget or forgive their . . . betrayal. . . . All knew that in Napoleon Bonaparte they had a commander in chief . . . who abandoned them to save his own skin."

Seizing Power

When Napoleon arrived in Paris, he found the nation in a state of chaos. Inflation had soared, the government was bankrupt, the French army in Italy had been forced to retreat from most of its conquests, and several anti-republican revolts had broken out in many parts of France. Napoleon saw the chaos as an opportunity to seize power. So he allied himself with a member of the Directory named Emmanuel-Joseph Sieyès, who was urging the creation of a new government with a strong executive at its top.

In November, under pressure from Sieyès, the Directory resigned. The legislature, alarmed by reports of a new radical uprising in Paris, moved from the Tuileries to a palace in the suburb of Saint-Cloud. In the meantime, Napoleon had been made commander of all Paris troops. After surrounding the palace in Saint-Cloud with soldiers, he planned to convince the upper house of the legislature to accept Sieyès's plan for a new government headed by three leaders called consuls. To his dismay, the legislators began shouting, "Down with dictators!" and "Bayonets don't frighten us!"

Trembling and incoherent, Napoleon was led outside by some of his aides. His brother Lucien then came to the rescue. He told the troops that the lawmakers were being terrorized by a group of lunatics and that an attempt had been made to assassinate Napoleon. The soldiers promptly set their bayonets and rushed

Lawmakers at Saint-Cloud shout down Napoleon as he urges them to change the government and install three consuls as rulers.

into the palace. The legislators promptly jumped out the windows and hid in the nearby bushes.

Several hours later, those legislators who could be relied on to vote for the new government were allowed back into the palace by the soldiers. The legislators agreed to replace the Directory with three consuls: Napoleon, Sieyès, and a man named Pierre Roger-Ducos. The First Consul—who would have all the power—was of course Napoleon.

Over the next few weeks, the three consuls drafted a new constitution. It was very different from the Declaration of the Rights of Man. Napoleon believed the French no longer cared about liberty or equality or individual rights. What most of them wanted, he felt, was for property to be protected and for everyone to have a chance to rise to the top.

In February 1800, the new constitution was presented to the French people for their approval. There was no secret ballot: you had to state your position openly. About half of the eligible voters did not go to the polls. Of those who did, roughly 3 million voted in favor of the new government, 1,500 against.

Napoleon was now master of France.

The First Consul

Napoleon moved swiftly to reorganize the country. On the economic front, he balanced the budget, forbade members of the government to take money for their own use out of the treasury, and established the Bank of France to reform the monetary system. On the political front, he divided France into ninety-eight administrative departments that were run from Paris. Even local mayors were chosen by the interior minister, who was appointed by Napoleon. Although a three-part national legislature was set up, only Napoleon and his close advisers had the right to introduce laws. The French government was now much more honest and efficient, but it was also much more centralized.

The government was also much more authoritarian. In fact, many historians have called Napoleonic France the first modern police state. Most of the country's newspapers were shut down. The few remaining newspapers could publish only news and articles that had been approved by government censors. Books and plays were likewise censored. A secret police force spied on private organizations and denounced anyone who spoke against Napoleon. Those who were denounced were often imprisoned without trial. The secret police also opened private letters and reported on what teachers said in their classrooms. The statement in the Declaration of the Rights of Man that every citizen might "speak, write, and print with freedom" was completely ignored.

Shortly after being named First Consul, Napoleon led a famous march across the Alps, through the Great Saint Bernard Pass and into the Po Valley of northern Italy. This picture, by Jacques-Louis David, France's best-known painter of the period, commemorates the event. You can read more about David on page 74.

Napoleon also reinstated slavery in France's overseas colonies.

Napoleon's longest-lasting administrative reform was the Napoleonic Code, which took effect in 1804. For centuries, the law had varied from place to place. For example, an act might be legal in one town but illegal in the next town. Napoleon named a commission to bring the country's laws together. He also presided over almost half of the commission's meetings and made numerous specific suggestions.

The Napoleonic Code was a political compromise. On the one

hand, it kept many revolutionary reforms. For example, the traditional privileges of the nobles and clergy were abolished. Peasants could keep the lands they had acquired during the revolution, even though those lands had been confiscated from the church and the nobility. People could practice whatever religion they wished. On the other hand, the Code contradicted the revolutionary goal of equality. For example, workers and tradespeople were not allowed to form unions. Workers had to carry identity cards. If there was a dispute between an employer and his labor force, courts were to believe the employer. Fathers received greater power over their children, including the right to have them imprisoned. Husbands received greater power over their wives. It became almost impossible for a woman to obtain a divorce. Nor was a woman allowed to sell or administer property.

Napoleon wanted to unify France after the years of rebellion and civil war. Accordingly, he invited those royalists who had fled the country to return home. More importantly, he resumed relations with the Roman Catholic Church. He himself was not religious, but he realized the importance of religion to the French people and to society as a whole. In 1801, Napoleon and Pope Pius VII signed an agreement known as the Concordat. It recognized Catholicism as France's majority religion. Although the state kept the church property it had seized during the revolution, church schools—which had been closed since then—were reopened, and the state agreed to pay the clergy's salaries.

The Empire Expands

For a generation after the revolution, France was almost continuously at war. The nations with whom it fought varied, and occasionally some of its enemies became allies. Its one constant enemy, however, was England. The reason was the Industrial Revolution. England had begun industrializing early. By the end of the 1700s, it was the greatest manufacturing nation in the world. However, its most important markets were in mainland Europe. If France were to dominate the continent, it could disrupt England's trade and severely damage its economy. Accordingly, England adopted a two-pronged strategy to prevent this from happening. Its navy enabled it to control the seas, while it organized various coalitions of European nations to fight against France on land.

The first war against France ended in March 1802, about a year after Napoleon recaptured northern Italy, which had fallen back into Austrian hands. The peace lasted just fourteen months. Napoleon—who by this time had been named First Consul for life—spent the time building a huge fleet of flatboats with which to invade England. He also sold the Louisiana Territory in North America to the United States for $15 million. For Napoleon, it was a good deal. It prevented the British from occupying the territory, and it brought the French treasury some sorely needed cash.

Soon after, a new war between France and England broke out. But before any major battles were fought, Napoleon took another step upward. In May 1804 he had himself proclaimed emperor of France.

The coronation took place six months later. It was a magnificent spectacle. More than eight thousand notables from all over Europe, including Pope Pius VII, crowded into the Cathedral of

The coronation of Napoleon and Josephine, from a portion of a painting by Jacques-Louis David. David received only two tickets to the event. Furious, he included his family and friends in the painting even though they had not been present at the ceremony.

Notre-Dame in Paris as cannons boomed in the city's streets. Napoleon and Josephine sat on golden thrones. Napoleon wore a gold and ermine robe and carried a sword supposedly wielded a thousand years earlier by Charlemagne. Josephine wore a white satin gown with a crimson velvet train and was bedecked with diamonds on her head, ears, and neck. The climax came when Napoleon, instead of being crowned by the pope as had been the custom in the past, placed the crown on his own head. He then crowned his wife.

In 1805, hostilities between France and England intensified. In October, a British fleet commanded by Admiral Horatio Nelson finally caught up with a combined French and Spanish fleet led by Admiral Pierre de Villeneuve. Nelson had chased Villeneuve for two years, over the Atlantic to the Caribbean and then back to Europe. Now the two fleets met off Trafalgar, a sandy cape on the Spanish coast near the Strait of Gibraltar. There Nelson, who had one blind eye and only one arm, repeated his earlier success at Abu Qir Bay. He destroyed two-thirds of the French-Spanish fleet without losing a single ship. Although Nelson was killed by a sniper's bullet, the battle of Trafalgar ended Napoleon's dream of invading England.

Two months later, in December, the situation was different. Napoleon defeated a Russian-Austrian army at Austerlitz. (Russia and Austria were allies of England.) Many historians consider this battle Napoleon's tactical masterpiece. He concealed his best troops in the rear and purposely weakened his right flank. The Russians and Austrians fell into the trap and attacked on the right. The concealed French soldiers then burst forth, split the attackers into three sections, and smashed each section in turn. Austria sued for peace, while the Russians withdrew within their own borders.

At this point, Prussia entered the fray against France. Once again, Napoleon's mastery of tactics gained him victory. He defeated the Prussians in two battles in October 1806. He now controlled most of Europe except for England and Russia.

Napoleon turned his attention first to England. Unable to invade her or defeat her at sea, he decided to try economic warfare. He forbade European countries to trade with her in the hope that would destroy her industry. This boycott is known as the Continental System. Unfortunately for Napoleon, it did not work well. For one thing, it required thousands of customs inspectors to be stationed at all the ports under French control. It also required thousands of soldiers to back up the inspectors and try to prevent smuggling. Smuggling, in fact, was the main result of the Continental System. Trade even continued between England and France. The English refused to give up French brandy and French silk. The French wanted the sugar, coffee, tea, and tobacco that came from England's overseas colonies, to say nothing of English cloth for army uniforms.

While setting up the Continental System, Napoleon also moved against Russia. The two nations' armies clashed in February 1807. The result was a draw, with heavy casualties on both sides. In June, however, Napoleon succeeded in defeating the Russians. The next month, he and Czar Alexander of Russia met aboard a raft on the Neman River near the city of Tilsit. Among other things, the Treaty of Tilsit created an alliance between France and Russia that would last until 1812.

The Empire Comes Apart

Napoleon often said that a general began to lose his ability to lead after a decade or so. His own career was a good example. He started his rise to glory in 1796. Eleven years later, he made the first of a series of mistakes that would eventually bring about his downfall.

The Peninsular War

In 1807, Napoleon decided to occupy Portugal, which had refused to join the Continental System. After receiving permission to march through Spain, French troops won a quick victory, and the Portuguese royal family fled. Napoleon then lured the king of Spain to France and locked him up. In his place, the emperor made his brother Joseph Bonaparte the new king of Spain. (Napoleon had previously placed other brothers on various European thrones and married his sisters to different rulers.)

On May 2, 1808, the inhabitants of Madrid, the Spanish capital, rose in revolt. Soon other Spaniards did the same. Unable to resist French troops in regular combat, they adopted what is now known as guerrilla warfare, from the Spanish word *guerrilla*, meaning "little war." As one historian described the new tactics, "Every day French detachments were ambushed, supply trains

Spanish guerrillas fought the French invaders in every way they could.

raided, individual soldiers sniped at or knifed. Food might be poisoned; a friendly host, giving shelter to some tired courier, might . . . murder him in his sleep; churches might be arsenals; priests might carry pistols concealed in their habits."

The French retaliated with mass executions and other atrocities.

Then the British landed troops in Portugal under the command of Arthur Wellesley, later and better known as the Duke of Wellington. The French were soon driven out of Portugal. The war in Spain, however, continued to drag on. It became marked by "commando raids" on the part of the British, who would stage lightning attacks against the French and then withdraw to safety. Napoleon kept sending more and more soldiers into Spain and even went there himself to lead his army. At this point Austria once again declared war on France.

The Austrian Connection

Napoleon decided that his eastern front was more important than his western front. After all, he thought, the guerrillas were bound to lose eventually! So he left Spain and in July 1809 defeated the Austrians for the fourth time. A few months later, to everyone's surprise, France and Austria not only signed a peace treaty, they agreed to become joined by marriage. Napoleon divorced Josephine and married Marie-Louise, daughter of the Austrian emperor.

The marriage was politically advantageous to both sides. It also had a personal meaning for Napoleon. There had been no children from his marriage to Josephine, and he desperately wanted a son and heir. Marie-Louise admittedly was neither pretty nor witty. But she *was* young—eighteen to Napoleon's forty—and her mother had had thirteen children. Besides which, she was an actual princess. Napoleon was so pleased about her rank that he hired a new tailor and shoemaker to make himself look more elegant. He even learned how to dance the waltz.

The couple were married in April 1810. About a year later, Marie-Louise gave birth to Napoleon-François-Charles-Joseph, Napoleon II. The infant was immediately proclaimed king of Rome. As for Josephine, Napoleon visited her frequently and wrote her numerous letters, each of them starting with the words "My Love."

Both Napoleon and Josephine were very upset about their divorce, which Napoleon considered politically desirable. The emperor granted Josephine a large yearly allowance, settled her debts, and allowed her to keep Malmaison, her beautiful country house.

The Russian Campaign

Napoleon's marriage to Marie-Louise upset Czar Alexander. He was afraid that a French-Austrian alliance against Russia was in the making. Then, in 1811, internal economic problems led the czar to withdraw from the Continental System and open his country's ports to British ships. Furious at this action, Napoleon decided to invade Russia and teach his erstwhile ally a lesson. It was the worst mistake of his life.

Napoleon launched his invasion on June 24, 1812. His army, which numbered more than 600,000 men, was the largest he had ever commanded. But once again, as he had in Egypt fourteen years earlier, he failed to consider the geography and climate of the country he was invading.

Instead of giving battle, the Russians retreated across their vast plains. As they did so, they carried out a "scorched earth" policy, burning crops and filling wells with soil. By July, Napoleon's Grand Army was short of food and water. Many soldiers deserted. Others were killed or captured by Cossacks, the elite cavalry warriors of the Ukraine and Russia, who were fiercely loyal to the czar. The intense summer heat, combined with the lack of forage, also took its toll. Thousands of horses dropped dead, and it became increasingly difficult to move artillery and ammunition. Typhus swept through the Grand Army, killing tens of thousands.

On September 7, 1812, the Russian army made a stand at the town of Borodino, about seventy miles from Moscow, the nation's capital. Although Napoleon managed to eke out a victory, his casualties were heavy. Furthermore, the Russian army did not surrender; it simply retreated again.

On September 14, having covered more than seven hundred miles, the Grand Army—now reduced to one-sixth its original size—finally entered the gates of Moscow. Napoleon had expected to receive the keys of the city in surrender. Instead he met with silence. Except for a few thousand sick and wounded, the Russian capital was almost completely deserted. That night, its wooden buildings began to burn. The blaze continued for five days despite the efforts of French firefighters. By the time it died out, more than two-thirds of Moscow had been reduced to ashes.

Over the next five weeks, Napoleon made several overtures to Alexander for a truce. But the czar refused to negotiate. "He would rather let his beard grow and eat potatoes with the [peasants] . . . he declared . . . than make peace as long as a single foreign soldier remained on Russian soil."

By mid-October, flakes of snow began to fall. On October 19, Napoleon reluctantly gave the order to retreat. He tried to take a different route from the one he had followed in his advance but was prevented from doing so by the Russians. So back the Grand Army went over a route almost completely lacking in food and water. Soldiers were reduced to eating their horses and dogs. By the end of October, the dread Russian winter had set in. Snows were heavy, and the temperature fell to 22 degrees below zero. The men of the Grand Army had no winter coats, boots, gloves, or hats. The road was soon littered with frozen corpses and lined with abandoned artillery and discarded loot. There were even episodes of cannibalism.

On November 28, the Grand Army—now down to 40,000 freezing, starving men—crossed the Berezina River, pursued by three Russian armies. Then, learning of an attempted coup against

The retreat of the Grand Army from Moscow was one of the greatest disasters in military history.

him, Napoleon repeated his behavior in Egypt. He abandoned his troops and rushed back to Paris. His soldiers were left to make their way home as best they could.

The War for Liberation

Upon returning to Paris, Napoleon put down the attempted coup. But he was in desperate straits. He had almost no soldiers left, and most of Europe was up in arms against him. To the southwest was Wellington, who by May 1813 had driven the French out of Spain and was poised at France's border. To the east were the Russians

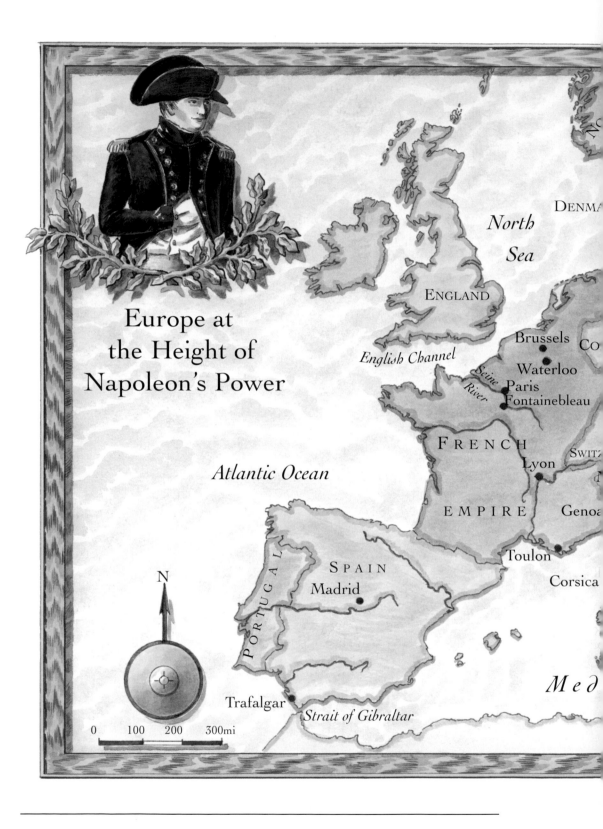

Europe at
the Height of
Napoleon's Power

North
Sea

DENMA

ENGLAND

English Channel

Brussels   Co

Waterloo
Seine   Paris
River   Fontainebleau

Atlantic Ocean

FRENCH   SWITZ

Lyon

EMPIRE   Genoa

Toulon

Corsica

N

PORTUGAL

SPAIN
Madrid

Me d

Trafalgar   Strait of Gibraltar

0   100   200   300mi

Moscow

Borodino

SWEDEN

Baltic Sea

Tilsit

Berezina River

Neman River

PRUSSIA

RUSSIA

Napoleon's Empire

Subject to Napoleon

Allies of Napoleon

Opposed to Napoleon

DUCHY OF WARSAW

UKRAINE

pzig

DERATION

THE

INE

Austerlitz

AUSTRIA

Black Sea

ND

Venice

ITALY

Adriatic Sea

OTTOMAN

EMPIRE

lba

Rome

KINGDOM OF SARDINIA

KINGDOM OF SICILY

erranean Sea

and the Prussians, joined in August by the Austrians. And to the north were the Swedes. All were allied against him.

Miraculously, Napoleon managed to raise another army, although its members were young and poorly trained. In October he fought a three-day battle against the allies at Leipzig (in what is now Germany). He won on the first day, although his troops suffered heavy losses and used up most of their artillery ammunition. On the second day, instead of regrouping and rearming, Napoleon did nothing. The only explanation historians give is that his health had been deteriorating for some time, and he was more lethargic and less decisive than he had ever been. On the third day, the allied forces defeated the French, and Napoleon was forced to retreat.

He refused to give up, however. Although the allied powers made several generous peace offers, he turned them all down. According to one historian, "He still believed in the force of his genius. He still believed in his empire. He still believed he could rally the French people."

Only he couldn't. On March 30, 1814, allied troops entered Paris. Three days later, the French senate declared that Napoleon was no longer emperor of France. On April 11, Napoleon accepted the inevitable and abdicated the throne. He was exiled for life to the island of Elba, near Corsica, and was promised an annual pension (which, however, he never received). Neither Marie-Louise nor his son was allowed to go with him, only a guard of several hundred men. Before leaving for Elba, Napoleon sent Josephine a note: "Good-bye, my dear Josephine, resign yourself, as I have had to do, and never forget him who has never forgotten you and never will." Josephine died eleven days later.

The "Hundred Days"

The allied powers replaced Napoleon with Louis XVIII, a younger brother of the late king Louis XVI. The new monarch was an easygoing man who was content to be a constitutional rather than an absolute ruler. He kept many of Napoleon's administrative and legal reforms. At the same time, he lifted Napoleon's restrictions on free speech and restored freedom of the press. However, he was very unpopular with several groups: peasants, radical republicans, and extreme royalists. Peasants who had bought land formerly owned by nobles and the Roman Catholic Church were afraid they would lose it. Radical republicans still supported the ideals of the revolution. Extreme royalists wanted their former lands and privileges restored.

On February 26, 1815, Napoleon escaped from Elba. He reached France three days later and immediately issued a proclamation to the French army:

> *Soldiers! In my exile I heard your voice. I have come back in spite of all obstacles and all dangers. Your general, called to the throne by the choice of the people and raised on your shields, is restored to you: come and join him. . . . Come and range yourselves under the flags of your leader! He has no existence except in your existence; he has no rights except*

your rights and those of the people; his interests, his honor,
his glory are none other than your interests, your honor, your
glory. Victory will march at a quickstep. The eagle and tri-
color [French flags] shall fly from steeple to steeple to the
towers of Notre Dame! Then you can show your scars with-
out dishonor, then you can pride yourselves on what you have
accomplished: you will be the liberators of the fatherland!

The appeal to nationalism, combined with "a nostalgic loyalty to the emperor," worked. Louis XVIII fled France, and on March 20 Napoleon entered Paris, just ten months after he had left. He immediately set to work raising a new Grand Army to resist the allied powers. The Austrian and Russian armies were still far away, but the Prussians and the British were close at hand in Belgium.

Napoleon struck first at the Prussians and drove them from the battlefield. Instead of dissolving, however, the Prussian army regrouped and circled around the French. In the meantime, Napoleon confronted the British near the village of Waterloo, a few miles south of the Belgian capital of Brussels. The British were commanded by the Duke of Wellington, who had learned a great deal about tactics during the Peninsular War in Portugal and Spain. He hid a large part of his army behind some rolling hills. This protected them from the opening bombardment by French cannons. Then, when the French infantry charged, the British soldiers rose from concealment and blasted away with their muskets. In the meantime, the Prussians reached the battlefield and began attacking the French from the rear.

By nightfall, Napoleon had lost his final battle. "A broken man," wrote one historian, "he raced back to Paris in tears. His return to power—the Hundred Days—was over."

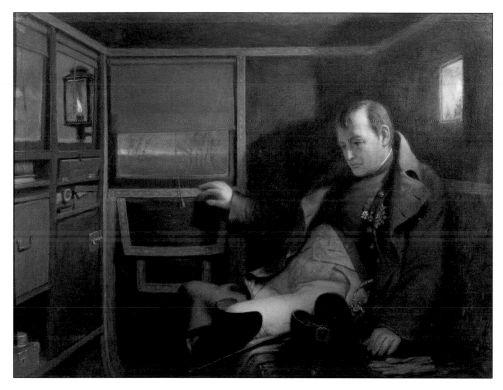

Ever since the Battle of Waterloo left Napoleon a broken man, people have used the expression "He met his Waterloo" to describe an individual's final defeat, whether in war, business, or politics.

For the second time, Napoleon abdicated the throne of France. He then considered seeking asylum in the United States. Instead, he was captured by the British and exiled to an even smaller and more desolate island than Elba: the island of Saint Helena, situated in the Atlantic Ocean some 1,200 miles off the west coast of Africa. There he spent the next six years, writing his memoirs and trying to justify himself and his actions in the eyes of the world.

On May 5, 1821, Napoleon died at the age of fifty-one. Doctors attributed his death to various causes, including ulcers, liver disease, and stomach cancer, which had killed his father and two of his sisters. In recent years, however, many historians have come to believe that Napoleon was murdered by a combination of arsenic and cyanide. The poison was thought to have been administered to him over a period of years by Count Charles Tristan de Montholon, one of the few men who had joined the former emperor in his exile.

Napoleon's body was placed in a mahogany coffin and buried on Saint Helena. The French wanted his tombstone to read "Emperor Napoleon." The British wanted it to read simply "Napoleon Bonaparte." The result was that Napoleon's grave went unmarked. In 1840, however, his body was brought back to Paris and given a final resting place of honor in the Hôtel des Invalides (a former home for disabled veterans that is now a military museum). The emperor's last wish was fulfilled. In his will, he had written that he wanted to be buried "on the banks of the Seine, amidst the French people whom I loved so well."

Napoleon's Legacy

Napoleon changed Europe in many ways. He created the first modern mass army, with officers promoted by merit rather than birth. He spread the revolutionary ideas of liberty and equality, even though he often failed to put them into practice. He permitted freedom of religion. He rebuilt much of Paris and turned it into a beautiful city filled with art. The Napoleonic Code became the basis of civil law throughout much of the European continent. The French people developed a strong sense of nationalism, of pride in being French. Many still look back on the Napoleonic era as the time of their country's greatest glory.

Some of Napoleon's actions had results he could not have foreseen. By combining small Italian states into larger ones, he laid the foundation for the unification of Italy in the late 1800s. He did the same for Germany. His creation of the Duchy of Warsaw led to the establishment of present-day Poland. His sale of the Louisiana Territory almost doubled the size of the United States and helped it become a powerful nation. Twentieth-century dictators such as Adolf Hitler, Joseph Stalin, and Mao Tse-tung imitated his system of government, with its concentration of power in a single authoritarian ruler.

Some historians praise Napoleon highly. Others condemn him. But all agree that he was a military genius and that his life was like a great novel of adventure.

PART TWO

A kitchen in a French
country house around 1814

Everyday Life in Napoleonic France

The Military

Napoleon believed in using a citizen army. Accordingly, every Frenchman—unless he was married, lacked an eye or a finger, or was rich enough to hire a substitute—was drafted for four years.

The main weapon employed by the French army was the flintlock musket. It measured five feet in length and had a bayonet attached to the end of the barrel. The musket was not a particularly satisfactory weapon. For one thing, it was not dependable. In rain or snow, the powder with which it was loaded got wet, which meant the musket would not fire. For another thing, it was not accurate. You had to fire an average of 250 shots before you hit your target. As a result, French infantrymen fought in large, tight groups at close range. As one historian explains, "With lots of bullets flying in the same direction at the same time, someone was bound to be hit." As soon as the enemy began to waver, Napoleon's soldiers would charge, using their bayonets for hand-to-hand combat.

The most powerful weapons of Napoleon's army were its cannons. These fired balls that could travel for a distance of one mile. The cannonballs were made of iron and weighed from four to twenty-eight pounds. Napoleon developed a new way of using cannons in battle. In the past, they had been scattered among the infantry. Napoleon massed his cannons in one place. The result was a concentrated barrage of artillery fire that devastated the

French soldiers charge with their bayonets at the ready.

enemy line. Once the cannons had completed their work, the
infantry moved in.

Napoleon's army included cavalry. The heavy cavalry, consisting
of "big men on big horses," functioned the way tanks do today.
Its main purpose was to smash an enemy's formation. Heavy
cavalrymen wore armor and carried long swords called sabers that
were good for thrusting. The light cavalry, which was not armored,
was used mostly for reconnaissance, or gathering information
about the movement of enemy troops.

Infantrymen wore wool uniforms with padded coats and felt or
leather hats. The uniforms were mostly dark blue. The coats,
however, were "trimmed with all the colors of the rainbow. They

dripped with yellow, red, or gold braid. Cuffs and lapels ranged from white to pink to green." The theory behind the trimming on the coats was that bright colors increased the wearer's pride—and therefore his courage.

French soldiers on campaign usually lived off the countryside. This meant taking food from the unfortunate civilians through whose lands they might be passing. Army supply trains could carry only a limited amount of food. Besides, an army could move faster without the burden of wagon trains. If a soldier wanted luxury items such as tobacco, brandy, or wine, he would buy it from the vendors, usually women, who traditionally trailed behind the troops. French soldiers were also responsible for replacing their uniforms when these were ruined in battle. Sometimes the only way to obtain fresh cloth was to strip it from the dead.

Unlike the situation before the French Revolution, promotion in Napoleon's army did not depend on a soldier's social background. What counted was his courage in battle. As a result, many of the army's highest officers came from the lower class. Other outstanding soldiers were appointed to an elite corps called the Imperial Guard. There, as one historian writes, "the pay was higher, the food was better, and uniforms were more imposing." Napoleon was also generous with pensions and awards of various kinds. Among the latter was the Legion of Honor, which he established in 1802. The medal of the Legion of Honor is still France's highest prize.

Probably the greatest danger for Napoleon's army was not enemy guns and soldiers but poor medical treatment. It was true that medical officers and aid stations moved along with the French troops. Nonetheless, doctors at that time actually knew little about medicine. They had no antiseptics to prevent infection. In fact, they did not even realize that infection is caused by dirt. They seldom washed either their hands or their instruments. The most common treatment for a leg or arm wound was amputation, and the only anesthetic for such an operation was a stiff drink.

If you were wounded in the stomach or chest, you weren't treated at all but were either shot by a fellow soldier or left to die on the battlefield. Linen for dressing wounds was often in short supply. So were ambulances for carrying the wounded off the battlefield. Hospitals were frequently improvised, which meant that beds were made of straw and sanitation was nonexistent. Hospital food was poor as well; a typical dish was a soup made from horse meat. Epidemics of typhus and dysentery broke out repeatedly.

Another problem for Napoleon's army was desertion. Historians estimate that only about half of those drafted for service were actually under arms. As one general commented, "If these desertions continue, there will be only the officer corps left to serve." The high desertion rate not only damaged the army. It also hurt the civilian population, for many of the deserters became beggars, brigands, or smugglers.

Yet despite these problems, Frenchmen in general were proud to serve in Napoleon's army. There was glory in being led by one of the world's greatest generals. Many soldiers also felt that they were "soldiers of liberty," fighting for their country and for the ideals of the French Revolution.

Education

France's educational system was divided both vertically and horizontally. That is, there was one set of schools for the elite and another set of schools for the masses. At the same time, some schools were run by the state, while others were run by the Roman

A schoolboy in Napoleonic France studies his lessons.

Catholic Church. In general, girls attended religious schools because Napoleon did not think they needed to have a public education.

The government paid little attention to primary schools. They were designed simply to teach reading and writing to youngsters who would spend their lives as servants, farmers, and laborers. Napoleon was far more interested in the lycées, or state secondary schools. Open only to boys, the lycées were established in 1802 to teach science, classical languages (Latin and Greek), logic, and rhetoric, or the art of persuasive speaking. Their purpose was to train students for jobs in the government and the army. Textbooks were selected by the government, which also licensed the teachers. The lycées were run along semi-military lines. Students wore uniforms and marched to their classes to the beat of drums.

Napoleon either set up or reorganized a number of universities. Under his rule, the École Normale, which was designed to train teachers for the lycées, also prepared young men for college-level teaching positions. The École Polytechnique became a military academy that emphasized the physical sciences.

Earning a Living

The vast majority of French people earned their living from the land. Some farmers owned fields outright. Others were sharecroppers, who gave their landlord up to half their produce in exchange for the right to farm. The rest were day laborers, who lost their jobs in the fall after the harvest was over. Women as well as men worked in the fields.

French agriculture was not very productive. Most farmers

French farmworkers harvest a fall crop of potatoes.

worked small farms of fewer than twenty acres. They still employed old-fashioned farming methods, such as letting a portion of the land lie fallow, or unplanted, every three years. They owned few cattle. This meant not only a lack of beef but also a lack of manure to use as fertilizer, which in turn kept the crop yield low.

Some French workers were skilled artisans. There were relatively few factories, except in textile-producing cities. There, spinners and weavers—many of them young children—worked twelve to fourteen hours a day at their machines. Most textiles, however, were still produced by a "cottage industry" of people who worked at home.

There were no department stores or shopping malls in Napoleonic France. People bought much of their food and other necessities at street stalls or from street vendors. Numerous small shops catered to people in the immediate neighborhood. As one historian wrote, "The corner-street grocer, the confectioner, the wine-merchant, the butcher, the baker, and the candle-stick maker all knew their clientele personally." While this made shopping a pleasant social experience, it also meant that women spent a great deal of time going from store to store.

Napoleon was concerned about unemployment. To create jobs, he organized an extensive system of public works. He had thousands of miles of new roads built. He had riverbeds deepened and countless bridges put up. Marshes were drained, and major canals were dug. There were new military fortifications, especially for seaports. There were huge warehouses in Paris for grain and wine, as well as new buildings for the stock exchange, the Bank of France, and the General Post Office. In exchange for receiving public jobs, the workers on such projects were not allowed to strike.

Food

One of the distinctive things about French eating habits during the Napoleonic period was the time of day at which meals were served. Well-to-do Parisians usually ate two breakfasts, the first when they got up and the second around ten or eleven o'clock. The first breakfast consisted of a cup of coffee or hot chocolate, sometimes accompanied by a pastry. The second breakfast included eggs and cold meat. Dinnertime depended on a person's social position and occupation. Craftspeople and small shopkeepers, for example, dined at two. Lawyers and other professional people waited until five or six. Dinners included roast meats, fish, dessert, ices, strong coffee, and liqueur. When dinner was served late, many people did not eat again for the day.

Rich Parisians often gave banquets that lasted as long as five hours. This kind of banquet was a formal affair. There was a place card at each setting, and several candelabra along the length of the table. In the center of the table frequently stood an elaborate concoction of sponge cake and sugar, often representing some historical event. The majordomo announced each dish as it was carried into the dining room. Meat dishes included grilled steak, chicken pie, roasted partridge, and leg of lamb. Fish dishes were smothered in rich sauces and were accompanied by sweets, cheeses, and nuts. Dishes were passed around three times, and a butler refilled your wine glass as soon as it was half empty.

Conversation was discouraged so that people could concentrate on their food.

The diet of peasants and poor people consisted mostly of bread and a few vegetables. The bread was made from wheat or rye. The flour contained a great deal of bran (ground-up grain husks) and

Lunchtime in the country. In this sentimental scene, the fowl get fed along with the children.

wheat germ and, as a result, was fairly nutritious. The most common vegetables were peas and beans. People ate them fresh in spring and summer. Dried, they went into the soups and stews that were eaten in winter. Meat was expensive, so it was served only on special occasions such as weddings or religious holidays.

The potato had been promoted by the French government in 1795 as an alternative to grain. At first peasants considered it fit only for pigs. Under Napoleon, however, it slowly began appearing on people's tables. Sugar beets, too, made their way into France at about this time, and several hundred sugar-refining plants were built throughout the country. Other new foods, however, such as rice, were not accepted.

Houses and Furniture

Before 1789, houses in Paris did not have numbers. Nobles and rich people felt they were sufficiently prominent not to need house numbers, while poor people dealt only with neighbors, who knew where they lived. After the revolution, an attempt was made to number houses according to districts. This was very confusing because whenever a street entered a different district, the numbers began again. Thus a street that passed through seven districts would have seven houses with the number three. In 1805, Paris adopted the modern system: each street received its own numbers for its full length, with odd numbers on one side and even numbers on the other side.

Parisian apartment houses were often inhabited by both rich and poor people. However, tenants were divided according to the floor on which they lived. The ground or street floor contained shops. Rich people lived on the first floor. Above them, in ascending order, came well-to-do people, salaried people, and workers. Poor people inhabited the upper stories. Only in later years, with the invention of the elevator and the spread of roof gardens, did the top floor, or penthouse, become the most desirable space.

Many of the new apartment houses that went up in Paris under Napoleon were both handsome and luxurious, with large rooms, floor-to-ceiling mirrors, and marble fireplaces. Unfortunately, they were poorly laid out and rather uncomfortable to live in. There were no back stairs, so everyone—tenants, servants, and tradespeople alike—went up and down the main staircase. As a result, it soon became badly worn and dirty. Bathrooms were no more than cubbyholes. Many apartments, in fact, contained only a basin and a water jug concealed behind a door. Toilets were usually found on the stair landing. Kitchens were likewise situated outside the apartment. And most rooms of an apartment opened into one another, making privacy more or less nonexistent.

The apartments also suffered from poor heating and lighting. Since rooms were large and ceilings high, drafts were common. The only source of heat was a log fire. This was comfortable if you were leaning against the mantelpiece, but it did little to warm the rest of the room. It also threw off a considerable amount of dust. Most lighting was provided by candles, and at least one was kept burning all night long. Gas lamps were saved for special occasions.

Furniture was built in what is called Empire style. Its lines were simple, but the wood and the decorations changed with the times. At first, the fashion was for highly polished ebony or mahogany, embellished with bronze or gilt objects such as griffins, crowns, and lions' heads to commemorate Napoleon's exploits in Egypt. After the Continental System made exotic wood from abroad less available, people shifted to using plain domestic wood painted white and decorated with ornaments of gold. Summer furniture was usually made from iron. Rich women often kept a harp or a grand piano in the drawing room.

Well-to-do peasants lived in houses made of stone, wood, or a mixture of straw and clay, with roofs of slate or tile. Such houses

Juliette Récamier reclines on an elegant Empire-style sofa in this portrait by Jacques-Louis David. Madame Récamier was one of the leaders of Parisian society. A beautiful woman, she hosted a salon at which writers, artists, and politicians gathered for dining, music, and conversation.

usually contained several rooms. Poor peasants, on the other hand, lived in one-room huts with dirt floors and thatched roofs. In winter, their sheep and goats often lived in the hut with them. The heat given off by the animals meant their owners could burn less firewood.

Clothes and Makeup

During most of Napoleon's reign, fashionable women dressed in what, like their furniture, came to be called Empire style. Dresses fell in straight lines to the ground and had high waists, low square necklines, and short puffed sleeves. At first the dresses were made of thin fabrics, such as muslin and tulle. After a while, thicker materials, such as silk and velvet, became popular, especially since Napoleon wanted to help the silk industry of Lyon. For shoes, women wore heelless sandals. Many fashionable women added color to their outfits by draping scarves of brightly colored silk over their shoulders.

The leading dressmaker of the Napoleonic period was a man named Leroy. He employed a large staff of fitters and seamstresses, who received not only a salary but also room and board. Leroy charged very high prices for his gowns, so he was able to save a large amount of money even though he spent almost every evening at the gambling table.

In winter, fashionable women wrapped themselves in furs, especially blue fox, ermine, silver fox, and lynx. The most coveted fur was chinchilla, which came from South America. It was so rare and costly that only four or five women in Paris were lucky enough to own a chinchilla wrap. As the weather turned warmer,

The Empire style spread from France to other parts of Europe. Here, Maria Walewska, a Polish countess, wears a fashionable gown of blue velvet trimmed in gold.

women replaced their furs with shawls of cashmere or wool.

Many stylish women wore their hair short and close to the head. They decorated their hair with ribbons and gems. At first women wore turbans or small hats. Gradually the hats grew larger and assumed a variety of shapes. They were usually made of straw, felt, or satin and ranged in style from toques—small brimless hats—to huge bonnets with projecting brims.

Fashionable women used a great deal of makeup. They plastered their faces and necks with white greasepaint and smeared brilliant rouge on their cheeks and lips.

Fashionable men dressed more simply than they had before the revolution. They wore tight knee breeches or trousers, flowing linen cravats (neck cloths), and jackets that stopped at the waist in front but had long coattails in back. The jacket was often the most vivid part of a man's outfit, for it was frequently embroidered in bright colors. Over this, men sometimes wore long coats that came almost to the floor. Their feet were shod in shoes or boots made of leather. Most men stopped wearing wigs or dusting powder on their hair, which had been the fashion for most of the 1700s.

Peasants and poor people dressed much the way they had for centuries. They wore garments of heavy wool or linen, usually dyed blue, gray, or green. Made at home by the women of the family, these clothes were worn until they wore out. Sturdy clogs were the typical footwear.

Literature and the Arts

Perhaps the greatest writer of the Napoleonic period was Anne-Louise-Germaine de Staël. In addition to two novels, she wrote on such topics as relationships between literature on the one hand and religion and law on the other hand. The best government, she argued, was a constitutional one that combined liberty with order. When her father maintained that dictatorship was necessary in wartime, she answered that "freedom was more important than victory." This, of course, was contrary to Napoleon's viewpoint, so in 1803 he forbade Madame de Staël to come within a hundred miles of Paris. She spent the next eleven-odd

Madame de Staël believed strongly in the importance of education in a democratic society.

years in Switzerland, Russia, and England. During this time, she wrote a book comparing German and French culture. The book so enraged Napoleon that he ordered the entire first printing destroyed. Madame de Staël returned to Paris after the emperor's downfall in 1814.

Napoleon wanted to make Paris the "art capital of the Western world." Accordingly, as his armies marched across Europe, they seized paintings and sculptures everywhere and shipped them to France. There they were exhibited in the Louvre in Paris, as well as in the new museums that Napoleon established in at least fourteen other French cities.

The emperor also organized numerous art competitions, especially in the field of architecture. He preferred monumental structures that resembled those of ancient Rome. The most imposing structure started during his reign was the Arc de Triomphe in Paris, which imitates the Arch of Constantine in Rome.

Napoleon appointed Jacques-Louis David as his court painter. David painted two famous pictures of Napoleon. *Bonaparte Crossing the Alps* (see page 33), completed in 1801, shows Napoleon on a horse galloping up a rocky mountainside. *The Coronation of Napoleon* (see page 36), as the other picture is commonly called, was completed in 1807. It shows more than a hundred people watching Napoleon as he prepares to place the imperial crown on Josephine's head. The only person who was upset by this painting was Cardinal Caprara, who complained because David had painted him without the wig he usually wore. Everyone else, including Napoleon, admired the painting tremendously.

Having Fun

With the end of the revolution, well-to-do French—especially Parisians—devoted much of their time to having fun. A popular activity was going out for dinner. Dozens of first-class restaurants had sprung up. They were founded by chefs who had previously worked for the nobility. But most nobles had either lost their lives in the revolution or had fled France for safety in England and other countries. Since the chefs could no longer earn a living cooking for private employers, they decided to cook for the public at large.

Another popular activity was dancing. Dance halls were opened in all sorts of large empty spaces. One Parisian dance hall was even opened in the cemetery of a church! In 1797, the waltz was introduced and quickly became the rage. Dance halls also served as places where young men and women would go hoping to meet a suitable mate.

Still another popular activity was going to the theater. People attended plays at least once a week, and sometimes more. Tickets were inexpensive, and the productions changed often. Since Napoleon preferred tragedy to comedy, works by such classic French playwrights as Corneille and Racine became staples. The plays were censored, however. Lines that might be interpreted as criticizing Napoleon's seizure of power were cut, while verses justifying his actions were added. A play about the death of Julius Caesar was, as one historian put it, "banished from the boards because the audience applauded the speeches of Brutus against dictatorship."

The leading actor of the Napoleonic period was the tragedian François-Joseph Talma. He was noted for delivering his lines in a free, natural manner and for insisting on realistic costumes. Napoleon so admired Talma's performances that he paid the actor's debts, gave him large sums of money, and frequently had him over for breakfast.

Theater performances usually began at six o'clock in the evening, although a few theaters did not open until seven. Performances were usually over by half past nine. This allowed the audience to return home through Paris's dark streets without fear of attack by robbers.

Managing a theater was not easy. Civil servants were entitled to free tickets, which lowered profits. Company members demanded high salaries, and many of them refused to play certain parts or would take off without notice. Napoleon finally instituted a penalty of several days in jail for actors and singers who did not show up when they were supposed to.

The greatest difficulty a theater manager confronted, however, was the audience. It was common practice to whistle and groan loudly if you did not like a performance. Actors frequently hired groups of people—known as claques—to applaud their appearances. If there were two competing actors in a play or opera, the two claques might attack one another with wooden clubs. Sometimes the disruption was so great that the curtain had to be rung down before the performance was over.

When they weren't attending a theatrical performance, eating out, or going dancing, Parisians enjoyed strolling about the city's

Parisians enjoy a meal at a local restaurant.

public gardens. Expanses of grass, flowers, and trees were sur-
rounded by a "muddle of shops." There were shops for jewelers,
tailors, milliners, booksellers, watchmakers, wig makers, and shoe
shiners. Cafés and restaurants served food and iced drinks, while
fireworks displays dazzled people at night. Some of the gardens
resembled present-day amusement parks. You could go up in a
balloon and come down in a parachute. You could watch a troupe
of acrobats, play billiards, or gamble in a gambling arcade.

Under Napoleon, many of the holiday celebrations that had
been abolished during the revolution came back into favor. On
New Year's Day, Parisians once again received hampers of pista-
chio nuts, sugared almonds, and other candies purchased from
confectioners such as the famous Berthelot. In mid-Lent, people
once again donned masks and attended balls.

PART THREE

Josephine bought the
country house of
Malmaison, situated on
the bank of the Seine
River near Paris, while
Napoleon was in Egypt.
The château included a
farm and three hun-
dred acres of orchards,
meadows, vineyards,
and woodland.

The French in Their Own Words

Napoleon was a prolific correspondent. Historians estimate that he wrote anywhere from a dozen to thirty letters a day every day of his adult life. During his early years, he wrote by hand. Later, he dictated most of his letters to secretaries.

The first letter below was written to the Directory in 1796, when Napoleon was in the field in Italy. The second letter was written in 1807 to Josephine from Finkenstein, a Polish palace where Napoleon was entertaining his favorite mistress, Maria Walewska. The third is a note the emperor wrote, also while at Finkenstein, in which he lays out his ideas for the establishment of a girls' school at Écouen, France.

To the Executive Directory
Headquarters, Brescia, 14th August 1796.

I think it worth while to give you my opinion of the generals serving with this army. You will see that very few of them are of any use to me.

Berthier: ability, energy, courage, character; everything in his favor.

Augereau: plenty of character, courage, firmness, energy; is accustomed to war, popular with his men, lucky in the field.

Masséna: active, tireless, enterprising, grasps a situation and makes up his mind quickly.

Serurier: fights like a soldier; dislikes responsibility; firm, has too poor an opinion of his men; an invalid.

Despinoy: dull, slack, unenterprising; doesn't understand war, is unpopular with his men, doesn't use his head;

in other ways a man of high character, intelligence, and sound political principles; good for a home command.

Sauret: *good, an excellent soldier; not enough education for a general; unlucky.*

Abbatucci: *not fit to command fifty men.*

Garnier, Meunier, Casabianca: *incapable; unfit to command a battalion on such an active and serious campaign.*

Macquart: *a good fellow; no ability; lively.*

Gaultier: *all right for a clerical job; has never seen a shot fired.*

Vaubois *and* Sahuguet *were on garrison duty, and have only just been listed for active service: I will try to form an opinion of them. They have done very well in the duties so far assigned them: but the example of General Despinoy, who did very well at Milan, and very badly at the head of his division, compels me to judge men by their actual performance.*

To the Empress

> *Finkenstein, 10th May 1807.*

I have received your letter. I don't understand what you say about my lady correspondents. There is only one person I love, and that's my little Josephine. She's kind, she's capricious, she easily takes offence. Her quarrels are as graceful as everything she does: for she is always adorable, except when she is jealous, and then she becomes a regular little devil. But to return to these ladies of yours. If I were to waste my time on any of them, you can be sure they would have to be as pretty as rose-buds. Does that fit the ladies you mean?

I want you never to dine with people who have not dined with me. Keep to the same list for your private parties. Never invite ambassadors or foreigners to Malmaison: I should be angry with you, if you did. And don't let yourself be imposed upon by people whom I don't know, and who wouldn't come to see you if I were there.

Good-bye, my dear. All my love.

✥

Note

Finkenstein, 15th May 1807.

What are the girls brought up at Écouen going to be taught? You must begin with religion in all its strictness. Don't allow any compromise on this point. Religion is an all-important matter in a public school for girls. Whatever people may say, it is the mother's surest safeguard, and the husband's. What we ask of education is not that girls should think, but that they should believe. The weakness of women's brains, the instability of their ideas, the place they will fill in society, their need for perpetual resignation [patient acceptance], and for an easy and generous type of charity—all this can only be met by religion. . . .

In addition, the girls must be taught writing, arithmetic, and elementary French, so that they may know how to spell; and they ought to learn a little history and geography: but care must be taken not to let them see any Latin, or other foreign languages. The elder girls can be taught a little botany, and be taken through an easy course of physics or natural history. . . .

I don't know whether it is possible to give them some idea of medicine and pharmacology, at any rate that kind of medical knowledge commonly required for nursing invalids. It would be a good thing, too, if they knew something about the work done in the housekeeper's room. I should like every girl who leaves Écouen, and finds herself at the head of a small household, to know how to make her own frocks, mend her husband's things, make clothes for her babies, provide her little family with such occasional delicacies as can be afforded by a provincial housekeeper, nurse her husband and children when they are ill, and know in these matters, because she has been taught it beforehand, what invalids have learnt by experience. . . .

I want to make these young persons into useful women, and I am sure that in that way I shall make them attractive wives.

A somewhat different attitude toward marriage is found in the personal columns that were common in French newspapers. The following items appeared in 1804.

A YOUNG LADY AGED THIRTY, WELL-BORN, WITH ONE THOUSAND SIX HUNDRED FRANCS AND SOME NICE FURNITURE, WISHES TO ENTER INTO A LEGAL UNION WITH A MAN OF GOOD MORALS, HAVING A SITUATION IN AN OFFICE OR SOMETHING TO LOOK FORWARD TO.

A WIDOWER WITH ONE THOUSAND FOUR HUNDRED FRANCS PER ANNUM, RESIDENT FOR THE LAST TEN YEARS IN A PLEASANT APARTMENT NEAR THE TUILERIES, SEEKS A LADY OF SUITABLE AGE, GOOD-TEMPERED, WITH SOME MEANS OF HER OWN, TO OFFER HER SUGGESTIONS THAT MAY SUIT HER, OR LISTEN TO HER OWN.

A catechism is a set of religious questions and answers that young Catholics are supposed to memorize. Following is an excerpt from a catechism published in 1808, written by Napoleon himself.

> QUESTION: *What are the duties of Christians toward the princes who govern them, and what, in particular, are our duties toward Napoleon I, our Emperor?*
>
> ANSWER: *Christians owe to the princes who govern them, and we, in particular, owe to Napoleon I, our Emperor, love, respect, obedience, loyalty, military service and the taxes ordered for the preservation of his Empire and his throne. . . .*
>
> QUESTION: *Why do we have these duties toward our Emperor?*
>
> ANSWER: *. . . Because God, who creates Empires . . . has set him up as our sovereign and made him the agent of His power, and his image on earth. So to honor and serve our Emperor is to honor and serve God himself. . . .*
>
> QUESTION: *What must one think of those who may fail in their duty toward our Emperor?*
>
> ANSWER: *According to the Apostle Paul, they would resist the established order of God Himself and would be worthy of eternal damnation.*

Much of our information about Napoleon's 1812 Russian campaign comes from a memoir written by Sergeant A. J. B. F. Bourgogne of the Imperial Guard. In the first excerpt below, he lists the items he had accumulated by the time he reached

Moscow. In the second excerpt, he describes an incident during the retreat from Moscow.

I found [in my knapsack] several pounds of sugar, some rice, some biscuit, half a bottle of liqueur, a woman's Chinese silk dress, embroidered in gold and silver, several gold and silver ornaments, amongst them a little bit of the cross of Ivan the Great—at least, a piece of the outer covering of silver gilt, given me by a man in the company who had helped in taking it down . . . a woman's large riding-cloak (hazel color, lined with green velvet . . .): then two silver pictures in relief, a foot long and eight inches high. . . . I had, besides, several lockets and a Russian Prince's spittoon set with brilliants . . . a large pouch hung at my side, underneath my cap, by a silver cord. This was full of various things—amongst them, a crucifix in gold and silver, and a little Chinese porcelain vase. . . . Add to all this a fair amount of health, good spirits, and the hope of presenting my respects to the Mongol, Chinese and Indian ladies I hoped to meet, and you will have a good idea of the . . . sergeant of the Imperial Guard.

❦

The Prince Emile of Hesse-Cassel was with us, and his contingent . . . about a hundred and fifty dragoons were left; but these were almost all on foot, their horses being dead and eaten. These brave men . . . sacrificed themselves in this awful night to save their young Prince, not more than twenty years of age. They stood round him the whole night wrapped in their great white cloaks, pressed tightly one against the other, protecting him from the wind and cold. The next morning three-quarters of them were dead and buried beneath the snow.

In addition to Madame de Staël, another great writer of the Napoleonic period was François-Auguste-René de Chateaubriand. He had supported Napoleon at first but became a bitter anti-Bonapartist after his brother was executed for treason. In 1814,

Although he savagely condemned Napoleon in his pamphlet, Chateaubriand considered the emperor one of the greatest men who ever lived.

Chateaubriand issued a political pamphlet in which he condemned the emperor's actions and called on the French people to welcome Louis XVIII as their ruler. The pamphlet circulated throughout France and was said by Louis XVIII to be worth 100,000 soldiers. In the following passage, Chateaubriand addresses Napoleon.

[The whole human race] accuses you, calls for vengeance in the name of religion, morality, freedom. Where have you not spread desolation? In what corner of the world is there a family so obscure as to have escaped your ravages? Spain, Italy, Austria, Germany, Russia demand of you the sons that you have slaughtered, the tents, cabins, châteaux, temples that you have put to flame. . . . The voice of the world declares you the greatest criminal that has ever appeared on the earth . . . you who in the heart of civilization, in an age of enlightenment, wished to rule by the sword of Attila [a warrior known as the Scourge of God who invaded the Roman Empire] and the maxims of Nero [a vicious Roman emperor]. Surrender now your scepter of iron, descend from that mound of ruins of which you have made a throne! We cast you out as you cast out the Directory. Go, if you can, as your only punishment, to be witness of the joy that your fall brings to France, and contemplate, as you shed tears of rage, the spectacle of the people's happiness.

The following headlines, which reportedly appeared in French newspapers during March 1815, follow Napoleon's movements after his escape from Elba.

9 MARCH: THE ANTHROPHAGUS [DEVOURER OF HUMANS] HAS QUITTED HIS DEN.

10 MARCH: THE CORSICAN OGRE HAS LANDED AT CAPE JUAN.

11 MARCH: THE TIGER HAS ARRIVED AT GAP.

12 MARCH: THE MONSTER SLEPT AT GRENOBLE.

13 MARCH: THE TYRANT HAS PASSED THROUGH LYONS.

14 MARCH: THE USURPER IS DIRECTING HIS STEPS TOWARDS DIJON.

18 MARCH: BONAPARTE IS ONLY SIXTY LEAGUES FROM THE CAPITAL. HE HAS BEEN FORTUNATE TO ESCAPE HIS PURSUERS.

19 MARCH: BONAPARTE IS ADVANCING WITH RAPID STEPS, BUT HE WILL NEVER ENTER PARIS ALIVE.

20 MARCH: NAPOLEON WILL TOMORROW BE UNDER OUR RAMPARTS.

21 MARCH: THE EMPEROR IS AT FONTAINEBLEAU.

22 MARCH: HIS IMPERIAL AND ROYAL MAJESTY YESTERDAY EVENING ARRIVED AT THE TUILERIES, AMIDST THE JOYFUL ACCLAMATIONS OF HIS DEVOTED AND FAITHFUL SUBJECTS.

Napoleon's view of himself can perhaps be seen best in "Advice to My Son," which was written shortly before the emperor's death.

My son . . . must always bear in mind the remembrance of what I have accomplished. . . . Such work as mine is not done twice in a century. I have been compelled to restrain and tame Europe with arms. . . . I have saved the Revolution as it lay dying. I have cleansed it of its crimes, and have held it up to the people shining with fame. I have inspired France and Europe with new ideas which will never be forgotten. May my son make everything blossom that I have sown! May he develop further all the elements of prosperity which lie hidden in French soil!

Glossary

artisan: A craftsperson, such as a weaver or goldsmith.

brigand: Someone who robs travelers.

brilliants: Precious gems, especially diamonds, cut with many facets so that they sparkle.

cavalry: A group of soldiers who fight on horseback.

châteaux: French castles or mansions.

coup d'état: A sudden, violent overthrow of a government.

czar: The ruler of Russia.

dragoon: A cavalryman, or soldier trained to fight on horseback.

forage: Grass and crops for horses and cattle to graze.

gilt: Covered with a thin layer of gold or silver; a thin layer of gold or silver.

guillotine: An instrument for cutting off people's heads that was used during the French Revolution after Dr. Joseph Guillotin recommended it as a quick, merciful means of execution.

infantry: A group of soldiers who fight on foot.

majordomo: The head butler or steward of a household.

radical: A person or group wanting extreme change in government or society.

rampart: A protective barrier.

scepter: A short staff held by a king or a queen to show authority.

For Further Reading

Blackburn, Julia. *The Emperor's Last Island: A Journey to St. Helena.* New York: Pantheon, 1991.

Carroll, Bob. *Napoleon Bonaparte.* San Diego: Lucent Books, 1994.

Henderson, Harry. *The Age of Napoleon.* San Diego: Lucent Books, 1999.

Herold, J. Christopher. *The Battle of Waterloo.* New York: American Heritage, 1967.

Marrin, Albert. *Napoleon and the Napoleonic Wars.* New York: Viking, 1991.

McGuire, Leslie. *Napoleon.* New York: Chelsea House, 1986.

Plain, Nancy. *Louis XVI, Marie-Antoinette, and the French Revolution.* New York: Benchmark Books, 2002.

Walter, Jakob. *The Diary of a Napoleonic Foot Soldier.* Edited by Marc Raeff. New York: Doubleday, 1991.

ONLINE INFORMATION*

http://www.napoleon-series.org
   More than 5,000 articles, maps, and other materials relating to Napoleon and his times.

http://www.napoleonic-literature.com
   A large collection of materials about Napoleon's life, including his will, some of his favorite sayings, and photos of his country house Malmaison.

http://www.napoleonic-alliance.com
   Several articles of interest, including "A Day in the Life of Napoleon."

http://www.napoleonguide.com
   More than 1,600 Web pages covering nearly every aspect of Napoleon's life and times.

*All Internet sites were available and accurate when this book was sent to press.

Bibliography

Auslander, Leora. *Taste and Power: Furnishing Modern France.* Berkeley: University of California Press, 1996.

Durant, Will, and Ariel Durant. *The Age of Napoleon: A History of European Civilization from 1789 to 1815.* New York: Simon and Schuster, 1975.

Haythornthwaite, Philip J. *Uniforms of the Napoleonic Wars.* Poole, Dorset, England: Blandford Press, 1973.

———. *The Napoleonic Source Book.* New York. Facts on File, 1990.

Herold, J. Christopher. *The Age of Napoleon.* New York: American Heritage, 1963.

Hibbert, Christopher. *Napoleon: His Wives and Women.* New York: W. W. Norton, 2002.

Johnson, Paul. *Napoleon.* New York: Viking Penguin, 2002.

Lewis, Gwynne. *Life in Revolutionary France.* New York: G. P. Putnam's Sons, 1972.

Marrin, Albert. *Napoleon and the Napoleonic Wars.* New York: Viking, 1991.

McGuire, Leslie. *Napoleon.* New York: Chelsea House, 1986.

McKay, John P., et al. *A History of Western Society.* Vol. 2: *From Absolutism to the Present.* 2nd ed. Boston: Houghton Mifflin, 1983.

Robiquet, Jean. *Daily Life in France under Napoleon.* Translated by Violet M. MacDonald. New York: Macmillan, 1963.

Schom, Alan. *Napoleon Bonaparte.* New York: HarperCollins, 1997.

Thompson, J. M., ed. and trans. *Napoleon's Letters.* New York: Dutton, 1954.

Notes

Part One: An Ambitious Man

Page 8 "quiet and solitary": Schom, *Napoleon Bonaparte*, p. 7.
Page 12 "speak, write, and print": Durant, *The Age of Napoleon*, p. 23.
Page 21 "Soldiers! You are ill-fed": Herold, *The Age of Napoleon*, p. 48.
Page 22 "Peoples of Italy!": Herold, *The Age of Napoleon*, p. 48.
Page 28 "the vast majority": Schom, *Napoleon Bonaparte*, p. 187.
Page 29 "Down with dictators!": Schom, *Napoleon Bonaparte*, p. 217.
Page 29 "Bayonets don't frighten us!": Schom, *Napoleon Bonaparte*, p. 217.
Page 39 "Every day French detachments": Herold, *The Age of Napoleon*, p. 194.
Page 44 "He would rather": Herold, *The Age of Napoleon*, p. 332.
Page 48 "He still believed": McGuire, *Napoleon*, p. 96.
Page 48 "Good-bye, my dear": Schom, *Napoleon Bonaparte*, p. 703.
Page 49 "Soldiers! In my exile": Herold, *The Age of Napoleon*, p. 368.
Page 50 "a nostalgic loyalty": Herold, *The Age of Napoleon*, p. 369.
Page 50 "A broken man": McGuire, *Napoleon*, p. 100.
Page 52 "on the banks of the Seine": Herold, *The Age of Napoleon*, p. 409.

Part Two: Everyday Life in Napoleonic France

Page 56 "With lots of bullets": Marrin, *Napoleon and the Napoleonic Wars*, p. 49.
Page 57 "Big men on big horses": Haythornthwaite, *Uniforms of the Napoleonic Wars*, p. 26.
Page 57 "trimmed with all the colors": Marrin, *Napoleon and the Napoleonic Wars*, p. 146.
Page 58 "the pay was higher": Herold, *The Age of Napoleon*, p. 163.
Page 59 "If these desertions continue": Lewis, *Life in Revolutionary France*, p. 152.
Page 59 "soldiers of liberty": Lewis, *Life in Revolutionary France*, p. 153.
Page 63 "the corner-street grocer": Lewis, *Life in Revolutionary France*, p. 109.
Page 73 "freedom was more important": Durant, *The Age of Napoleon*, p. 289.
Page 74 "art capital": Durant, *The Age of Napoleon*, p. 279.
Page 75 "banished from the boards": Durant, *The Age of Napoleon*, p. 287.
Page 77 "muddle of shops": Robiquet, *Daily Life in France under Napoleon*, p. 134.

Part Three: The French in Their Own Words

Page 80 "To the Executive Directory": Thompson, *Napoleon's Letters*, pp. 54–55.
Page 81 "To the Empress": Thompson, *Napoleon's Letters*, p. 180.
Page 82 "Note": Thompson, *Napoleon's Letters*, pp. 180–182.
Page 83 "A young lady": Robiquet, *Daily Life in France under Napoleon*, p. 150.
Page 83 "A widower": Robiquet, *Daily Life in France under Napoleon*, p. 150.
Page 84 "QUESTION: What are the duties": Marrin, *Napoleon and the Napoleonic Wars*, p. 102.
Page 85 "I found [in my knapsack]": Haythornthwaite, *The Napoleonic Source Book*, p. 275.
Page 85 "The Prince Emile": Haythornthwaite, *The Napoleonic Source Book*, p. 279.
Page 87 "[The whole human race] accuses you": Durant, *The Age of Napoleon*, p. 321.
Page 88 "9 March: The Anthrophagus": Haythornthwaite, *The Napoleonic Source Book*, p. 312.
Page 89 "My son": Durant, *The Age of Napoleon*, pp. 767–768.

Index

Page numbers for illustrations are in **boldface.**

Alexander of Russia, Czar, 38, 43, 44
army, French, 9, 14, 84
  in Egyptian campaign, 24, 25, **26**, 27–28
  in Italian campaign, 21–22
  life in the military, 56–59, **57**
  Napoleon abandons his troops, 27–28, **28**, 45
  and Napoleon's escape from Elba, 49–50
  and Napoleon's seizure of power, 29, 31
  in Russian campaign, 43–45, **45**
Austria
  alliance against France, 13–14
  Italian rule under, 21, 22
  Napoleon's defeat of, 37–38
  Napoleon's marriage to Marie-Louise, 41–42

Barras, Paul de, 18–19, 20
Bastille, fall of the, 12, **13**
Bonaparte, Joseph (brother), 39
Bonaparte, Lucien (brother), 29
Bonaparte, Napoleon, 4–5, **4**, **7**
  abdication and exile, 48, 51
  at war with England, 17–18, 35–36, 37
  birth of Napoleon II, 42
  death of, 51–52
  defeat of Austria and Russia, 37–38
  divorces Josephine, 41, **42**
  during French Revolution, 17–20

early military years, 8–9, **9**
Egyptian campaign, 24, 25, **26**, 27–28, **28**
emperor of France, 36–37, **36**, 74
as First Consul, 31, 32–34, **33**, 35
the "Hundred Days," 49–50, **51**
Italian campaign, 21–24, **23**
legacy of, 53
"Little Corporal" nickname, 22
marriage to Josephine, 20
marriage to Marie-Louise, 41–42, 43
military promotions, **17**, 18, 20
museums created by, 74
and Peninsular War, 39–41, **40**
Russian campaign, 43–45, **45**, 84–85
seizes power, 29, **30**, 31
writings of, 80–84, 89

Champollion, Jean-François, 27
Chateaubriand, François-Auguste-René de, 86–87, **86**
clothing and makeup, French, 70, **71**, 72
Committee of Public Safety, 14
Concordat, 34
consuls, 29, 31
  First Consul, 31, 32–34, **33**, 35
Continental System, 38, 39, 43, 68
Corsica

Napoleon flees Corsica, 17
Napoleon's birthplace, 8, **9**
Cossacks, 43
coup d'etat, 16, 44–45

dance halls, 75
David, Jacques-Louis, 74
  paintings by, **33**, **36**, **69**, 74
de Staël, Anne-Louise-Germaine, 73–74, **73**, 86
Declaration of the Rights of Man and of the Citizen, 12–14, 31, 32
Directory, the, 15–16, 20, 21, 22–24, 29, 31

educational system, France's, 60–61, **60**
Egyptian campaign, 24, 25, **26**, 27–28, **28**
Elba, island of, Napoleon's exile to, 48, 49, 88
Empire style furniture and clothing, 68, **69**, 70, **71**
England
  Battle of Waterloo, 50, 51
  and France in Egyptian campaign, 24, 25, 27–28
  and the Industrial Revolution, 35
  trade between France and, 38
  wars against France, 14, 17–18, 35–36, 37
Estates-General (French parliament), 11, 15

farm workers, French, 62–63, **62**

First Estate, 11, 12
first French Republic, 14–15
food
   French eating habits,
      64–65
   French kitchen, **54–55**
   French restaurants, 75,
      77
   for French soldiers, 21,
      58, 59
   peasant diet, 65–66, **65**
   street vendors, 63
French Revolution, 9, 10–12,
   10, **11**, **13**, 58, 59
   constitutional monarchy,
      12–14
   the Directory, 15–16, **15**
   first French Republic,
      14–15

gardens, public, 77
government, French,
      reorganization of,
      32–34
guerrilla warfare, 39–40, **40**
guillotine, 15, **15**, 18

holiday celebrations, 77
Hôtel des Invalides, 52
houses and furniture,
      French, **54–55**, 67–69,
      69, **78–79**

Industrial Revolution, 35
Italian campaign, 21–24, **23**

Josephine (Marie-Josèphe-
      Rose de Beauharnais),
      18, **19**
   country home, 42, **78–79**
   death of, 48
   empress of France,
      36–37, **36**, 74
   marriage and divorce to
      Napoleon, 20, 41, **42**

Legion of Honor, 58
Leroy (dressmaker), 70
literature and the arts,

French, 73–74, **73**
Louis XVI (France), 11, **11**,
   12, 25, 49
Louis XVIII (France), 49,
   50, 87
Louisiana Territory, 35, 53
lycées (schools), 61

Marie-Antoinette (queen of
   France), **10**
Marie-Louise (Austrian
   princess), 41–42, 43, 48
men's clothing, 72
Montholon, Charles Tristan
   de, 52

Napoleon II (Napoleon-
   François-Charles-
   Joseph), 42, 48
Napoleonic Code, 33–34,
   53
National Assembly, French, 12
National Convention,
   French, 14, 15–16, 18
nationalism, French, 50, 53
Nelson, Horatio, 25, 37
nobles, French, 10–11

Oath of the Tennis Court, 12
Ottoman Empire, 24, 27

peasants, French, 49
   diet of, 65–66, **65**
   peasant clothing, 72
   peasant housing, 68–69
Peninsular War, 39–41, **40**,
   50
Pius VII, Pope, 34, 36
playwrights, French, 75
Portugal, Napoleon's
   occupation of, 39, 41
Prussia
   alliance against France,
      13–14
   defeats Napoleon, 50
   Napoleon's defeat of, 38
public works system,
   France's, 63

radical republicans, 49

Reign of Terror, 15, 18
religion
   clergy, 10–11
   French Catholicism, 10,
      34
   Napoleon's catechism, 84
   religious schools, 60–61
Robespierre, Maximilien,
   14, 15, 18
Roger-Ducos, Pierre, 31
Rosetta Stone, 26–27
royalists, French, 14, 16,
   17, 19, 34, 49
Russia
   Napoleon's defeat of
      Austria and, 37–38
   Russian campaign,
      43–45, **45**, 84–85

Saint Helena, island of,
      Napoleon's exile to, 51
Second Estate, 11, 12
Sieyès, Emmanuel-Joseph,
   29, 31
Spain, wars against France,
   14, 17–18, 39–40, **40**,
   41, 45

Talma, François-Joseph, 76
theater performances,
   75–76
Third Estate, 11–12
Trafalgar, Battle of, 37
Treaty of Tilsit, 38
typhus, 43, 59

Villeneuve, Pierre de, 37

War for Liberation, 45, 48
Waterloo, Battle of, 50, 51
Wellesley, Arthur (Duke of
   Wellington), 41, 45, 50
women, French
   clothing and makeup,
      70, **71**, 72
   literature and the arts,
      73–74, **73**, 86
   in Parisian society, **69**, **71**
   women's rights, 34

About the Author

"As far back as I can remember, I have been interested in people who came before me—how they lived, what they thought, and what their leaders were like. The desire to know and understand is probably one reason why my favorite reading is mysteries, especially those set in ancient times and different cultures."

In addition to reading mystery novels, Miriam Greenblatt acts in community theater and is an avid adventure traveler. She has rafted rivers in Sumatra and Papua New Guinea, ridden a camel in India and an elephant in Thailand, and explored cities from Tokyo to Timbuktu. She is the author of several history textbooks, three presidential biographies for teenagers, and twelve titles in the Rulers and Their Times series. She lives in a northern suburb of Chicago with her two cats, Batu Khan and Barnum.